THIS BOOK BELONGS TO

_____

START DATE

_____

SHE READS TRUTH

FOUNDERS

FOUNDER
Raechel Myers

CO-FOUNDER
Amanda Bible Williams

EXECUTIVE

CHIEF EXECUTIVE OFFICER
Ryan Myers

CHIEF BRAND & MARKETING OFFICER
Amy Dennis

CHIEF OPERATING OFFICER
Raechel Myers

EDITORIAL

MANAGING EDITOR
Lindsey Jacobi, MDiv

PRODUCTION EDITOR
Hannah Little, MTS

ASSOCIATE EDITOR
Kayla De La Torre, MAT

COPY EDITOR
Becca Owens, MA

MARKETING

SENIOR MARKETING MANAGER
Katie Bevels

MARKETING PROJECT COORDINATOR
Kyndal Kearns

GROWTH MARKETING MANAGER
Blake Showalter

PRODUCT MARKETING MANAGER
Whitney Hoffman

CONTENT MARKETING STRATEGIST
Tameshia Williams, ThM

CREATIVE

DESIGN MANAGER
Kelsea Allen

ART DIRECTORS
Annie Glover
Lauren Haag

DESIGNER
Ashley Phillips

JUNIOR DESIGNER
Jessie Gerakinis

OPERATIONS

OPERATIONS DIRECTOR
Allison Sutton

OPERATIONS MANAGER
Mary Beth Steed

SHIPPING

SHIPPING MANAGER
Marian Byne

FULFILLMENT LEAD
Kajsa Matheny

FULFILLMENT SPECIALISTS
Hannah Lamb
Kelsey Simpson

SUBSCRIPTION INQUIRIES
orders@shereadstruth.com

COMMUNITY SUPPORT

COMMUNITY SUPPORT MANAGER
Kara Hewett, MOL

COMMUNITY SUPPORT SPECIALISTS
Katy McKnight
Alecia Rohrer
Heather Vollono

CONTRIBUTORS

SPECIAL THANKS
Taylor Krupp
Jessica Lamb

SHE READS TRUTH™

© 2024 by She Reads Truth, LLC

ISBN 978-1-952670-91-6

1 2 3 4 5 6 7 8 9 10

All Scripture is taken from the Christian Standard Bible®. Copyright © 2020 by Holman Bible Publishers. Used by permission. Christian Standard Bible® and CSB® are federally registered trademarks of Holman Bible Publishers.

Research support provided by Logos Bible Software™. Learn more at logos.com.

@SHEREADSTRUTH

 Download the She Reads Truth app, available for iOS and Android

  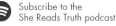 Subscribe to the She Reads Truth podcast

This book was printed offset in Nashville, Tennessee, on 70# Lynx Opaque. Cover is 100# Cougar Opaque with a soft touch lamination.

SHEREADSTRUTH.COM

PEOPLE OF REMEMBRANCE

A STUDY OF THE BIBLICAL PRACTICE OF REMEMBERING

SHE READS TRUTH

I NEEDED TO REMEMBER
SO I WOULD NOT FORGET.

Lindsey

Lindsey Jacobi, MDiv
MANAGING EDITOR

I remember vividly the season of transition after I made a right-but-hard decision to leave a familiar place with familiar people doing familiar work. I was left in the lurch of the in-between, not yet having the "next thing." What I did have was plenty of questions, "opportunity," time to (over)think, doubt about God's faithfulness to provide, concerns about finances, and worry about how much of a burden I was to the people who had chosen to catch me.

Looking forward was overwhelming. And so unclear. But when I had shoved all my belongings into a storage unit for an undetermined period of time, I made sure to grab the last few years' worth of prayer journals. I would just read and reread, scouring them for all the evidence I could find that this wasn't going to be the time that God left me out to dry. Because almost on a daily basis, that lie would creep in. *What if this is the time He doesn't come through? What if I made the wrong choice? What if I just flounder, never really finding the future God has for me?*

Thankfully, several people in the Bible also faced this seemingly universal reality of uncertain futures. They too needed kind and consistent reminders from the past. In this reading plan we'll see how throughout Scripture, remembrance brings the past reality of who God is and what He has done to bear in the present. To let it inform how we respond, live, repent, and walk with God. For me, reading those old journals became an act of stacking little stones of remembrance like the ones God told Joshua to set up on the far side of a dried-up Jordan River (more on that on Day 4!). I needed to keep in front of me those reminders of all the things I had known to be true in the past, and the specific ways I had seen God's character play out in my life. I needed to remember so I would not forget.

This is our hope and prayer as you journey through this reading plan. That God would bring to your mind what has been and remains true of Him: the universal and unique ways you have seen Him remain true to His character. That these ancient words would become stones of remembrance for your forgetful heart. And that you would find stable footholds in the tangible practices He has graciously given for His children to be reminded of this truth: He has never forgotten us.

DESIGN ON PURPOSE

At She Reads Truth, we believe in pairing the inherently beautiful Word of God with the aesthetic beauty it deserves. Each of our resources is thoughtfully and artfully designed to highlight the beauty, goodness, and truth of Scripture in a way that reflects the themes of each curated reading plan.

For this book, we used mirrors and their reflective properties to demonstrate the powerful effect remembering has in our relationship with God. In using light as the object of the mirror's reflection, these images point us to God's light reflected in and through us when we remember His faithfulness and goodness.

Abalone shells are another reflective material featured throughout the book. Instead of reflecting a mirror image, these shells become iridescent and colorful when light hits their surface. These images symbolize the new light and perspective the act of remembering brings to our hearts.

This book's soft and subtle color palette points us to the thoughtful and intentional act of remembering that trains our eyes on God's past work, so that we can reflect His loyal love to the world.

DESIGN ON PURPOSE

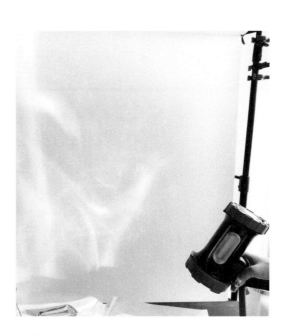

ABCDEFGHIJKLMN
OPQRSTUVWXYZ

LIGHT POURING ONTO BROKEN PIECES

ABCDEFGHIJKLMN
OPQRSTUVWXYZ

NEW IMAGES MADE FROM BROKEN PIECES

HOW TO USE THIS BOOK

She Reads Truth is a community of women dedicated to reading
the Word of God every day. In this **People of Remembrance**
reading plan, we will read a collection of scriptures that point
us to remember who God is and what He has done, how
He remembers us, and how we can be obedient to practice
remembrance in our own lives.

READ & REFLECT

Your **People of Remembrance**
book focuses primarily on
Scripture, with added features
to come alongside your time
with God's Word.

SCRIPTURE READING

Designed for a Monday start, this
book presents daily readings on
remembrance.

 *Supporting passages are marked
in your daily reading with the Going
Deeper heading.*

RESPONSE

Each week features questions and
space for personal application of the
week's reading.

COMMUNITY & CONVERSATION

You can start reading this book at any time!
If you want to join women from Hartford to
Hungary as they read along with you, the
She Reads Truth community will start Day 1
of **People of Remembrance** on Monday,
February 12, 2024.

SHE READS TRUTH APP

Devotionals corresponding to each daily reading can
be found in the **People of Remembrance** reading plan
on the She Reads Truth app. New devotionals will be
published each weekday once the plan begins on Monday,
February 12, 2024. You can use the app to participate in
community discussion and more.

GRACE DAY

Use Saturdays to catch up on your reading, pray, and rest in the presence of the Lord.

WEEKLY TRUTH

Sundays are set aside for Scripture memorization.

See tips for memorizing Scripture on page 100.

EXTRAS

This book features additional tools to help you gain a deeper understanding of the text.

Find a complete list of extras on page 10.

SHEREADSTRUTH.COM

The **People of Remembrance** reading plan and devotionals will also be available at SheReadsTruth.com as the community reads each day. Invite your family, friends, and neighbors to read along with you!

SHE READS TRUTH PODCAST

Subscribe to the She Reads Truth podcast and join our founders and their guests each week as they talk about what you'll read in the week ahead.

*Podcast episodes 212–214 for our **People of Remembrance** series release on Mondays beginning February 12, 2024.*

TABLE OF CONTENTS

I WILL REMEMBER THE LORD'S WORKS; YES, I WILL REMEMBER YOUR ANCIENT WONDERS. I WILL REFLECT ON ALL YOU HAVE DONE AND MEDITATE ON YOUR ACTIONS.

PSALM 77:11–12

INTRODUCTION

REMEMBRANCE IN SCRIPTURE

Zakar is the main Hebrew verb used in the Old Testament for concepts related to remembrance and memory. While the word does mean to recall the past, it also carries a greater weight—zakar involves doing something with our memories, using the past to inform our present thoughts, feelings, and actions. The New Testament uses the Greek word *mimnēskomai* to communicate the similar idea of allowing a past truth or reality to inform present action.

THE IMPORTANCE OF REMEMBRANCE

Most of us have a chronic case of spiritual amnesia—we all too easily forget who God is and what He has done. But what exactly is at stake if we forget? As we will see in our readings throughout this plan, God knows how our forgetfulness takes away from the abundant life that He alone can give. When we forget, we can more easily drift away from His Word and ways, stumbling headlong into disobedience. We settle for what the world offers instead of a life of flourishing with God.

The weight of remembering isn't always easy. When pain from the past lingers too long, we can become weary with our memories and prefer to forget. On the other hand, to forget the pain is also to forget the joys. Our highs have no reference point apart from the low places.

There is a discipline in remembering. It is a daily choice to let God's past faithfulness shape and steer our thoughts, prayers, habits, affections, decisions, and relationships. And when our reality feels unstable and uncertain, there is a solid, steadying weight in remembering that helps us see Him more clearly in the present.

IN THIS READING PLAN

This reading plan is a reminder of that truth, and how we see Scripture call us back again and again to who God is and what He has done. Remembering is a formative practice that involves both mentally recalling what is true and participating in tangible acts that ground us and move us forward in faith.

We will explore the biblical pattern of remembrance by reflecting on God's call for us to remember His faithfulness, God's people calling on Him to remember His promises, and the tangible practices of remembrance throughout Scripture. As you go, you'll have opportunities to reflect and respond in practical ways, building a rhythm of remembrance in your own life.

REMEMBERING

WEEK

01

GOD

From the earliest days, God established practices of remembrance for His people. From a rainbow after receded flood waters, to unleavened bread, to rocks gathered from a dried river bed, God gave His people tangible and regular signs and practices to serve as reminders of His faithfulness to His promises. Each one of these practices of remembrance prepared His people for the Son's coming.

In this week's readings, we will remember God's pattern of covenant loyalty, and His repeated call for His people to remember and act according to His ways.

REMEMBER GOD'S PROMISES

DAY 01

"I will confirm my covenant that is between me and you and your future offspring throughout their generations."

GENESIS 17:7

GENESIS 17:1–19

Covenant Circumcision

[1] When Abram was ninety-nine years old, the Lord appeared to him, saying, "I am God Almighty. Live in my presence and be blameless. [2] I will set up my covenant between me and you, and I will multiply you greatly."

[3] Then Abram fell facedown and God spoke with him: [4] "As for me, here is my covenant with you: You will become the father of many nations. [5] Your name will no longer be Abram; your name will be Abraham, for I will make you the father of many nations. [6] I will make you extremely fruitful and will make nations and kings come from you. [7] I will confirm my covenant that is between me and you and your future offspring throughout their generations. It is a permanent covenant to be your God and the God of your offspring after you. [8] And to you and your future offspring I will give the land where you are residing—all the land of Canaan—as a permanent possession, and I will be their God."

[9] God also said to Abraham, "As for you, you and your offspring after you throughout their generations are to keep my covenant. [10] This is my covenant between me and you and your offspring after you, which you are to keep: Every one of your males must be circumcised. [11] You must circumcise the flesh of your foreskin to serve as a sign of the covenant between me and you. [12] Throughout your generations, every male among you is to be circumcised at eight days old—every male born in your household or purchased from any foreigner and not your offspring. [13] Whether born in your household or purchased, he must be circumcised. My covenant will be marked in your flesh as a permanent covenant. [14] If any male is not circumcised in the flesh of his foreskin, that man will be cut off from his people; he has broken my covenant."

[15] God said to Abraham, "As for your wife Sarai, do not call her Sarai, for Sarah will be her name. [16] I will bless her; indeed, I will give you a son by her. I will bless her, and she will produce nations; kings of peoples will come from her."

[17] Abraham fell facedown. Then he laughed and said to himself, "Can a child be born to a hundred-year-old man? Can Sarah, a ninety-year-old woman, give birth?" [18] So Abraham said to God, "If only Ishmael were acceptable to you!"

[19] But God said, "No. Your wife Sarah will bear you a son, and you will name him Isaac. I will confirm my covenant with him as a permanent covenant for his future offspring."

GENESIS 26:23–25

The Lord Appears to Isaac

[23] From there he went up to Beer-sheba, [24] and the Lord appeared to him that night and said, "I am the God of your father Abraham. Do not be afraid, for I am with you. I will bless you and multiply your offspring because of my servant Abraham."

[25] So he built an altar there, called on the name of the Lord, and pitched his tent there. Isaac's servants also dug a well there.

GENESIS 35:9–15

[9] God appeared to Jacob again after he returned from Paddan-aram, and he blessed him. [10] God said to him, "Your name is Jacob; you will no longer be named Jacob, but your name will be Israel." So he named him Israel. [11] God also said to him, "I am God Almighty. Be fruitful and multiply. A nation, indeed an assembly of nations, will come from you, and kings will descend from you. [12] I will give to you the land that I gave to Abraham and Isaac. And I will give the land to your future descendants." [13] Then God withdrew from him at the place where he had spoken to him.

[14] Jacob set up a marker at the place where he had spoken to him—a stone marker. He poured a drink offering on it and poured oil on it. [15] Jacob named the place where God had spoken with him Bethel.

◖ GOING DEEPER

1 CHRONICLES 16:14–18

[14] He is the Lord our God;
his judgments govern the whole earth.

[15] Remember his covenant forever—
the promise he ordained for a
   thousand generations,

[16] the covenant he made with Abraham,
swore to Isaac,
[17] and confirmed to Jacob as a decree,
and to Israel as a permanent covenant:
[18] "I will give the land of Canaan to you
as your inherited portion."

GALATIANS 3:29

And if you belong to Christ, then you are Abraham's seed, heirs according to the promise.

ROMANS 4:20–21

[20] He did not waver in unbelief at God's promise but was strengthened in his faith and gave glory to God, [21] because he was fully convinced that what God had promised, he was also able to do.

"I WILL REMEMBER MY COVENANT BETWEEN ME AND YOU AND ALL THE LIVING CREATURES."

GENESIS 9:15

REMEMBER GOD'S MERCY

GENESIS 6:11–22

[11] Now the earth was corrupt in God's sight, and the earth was filled with wickedness. [12] God saw how corrupt the earth was, for every creature had corrupted its way on the earth. [13] Then God said to Noah, "I have decided to put an end to every creature, for the earth is filled with wickedness because of them; therefore I am going to destroy them along with the earth.

[14] "Make yourself an ark of gopher wood. Make rooms in the ark, and cover it with pitch inside and outside. [15] This is how you are to make it: The ark will be 450 feet long, 75 feet wide, and 45 feet high. [16] You are to make a roof, finishing the sides of the ark to within eighteen inches of the roof. You are to put a door in the side of the ark. Make it with lower, middle, and upper decks.

[17] "Understand that I am bringing a flood—floodwaters on the earth to destroy every creature under heaven with the breath of life in it. Everything on earth will perish. [18] But I will establish my covenant with you, and you will enter the ark with your sons, your wife, and your sons' wives. [19] You are also to bring into the ark two of all the living creatures, male and female, to keep them alive with you. [20] Two of everything—from the birds according to their kinds, from the livestock according to their kinds, and from the animals that crawl on the ground according to their kinds—will come to you so that you can keep them alive. [21] Take with you every kind of food that is eaten; gather it as food for you and for them." [22] And Noah did this. He did everything that God had commanded him.

GENESIS 7:11–16

The Flood

[11] In the six hundredth year of Noah's life, in the second month, on the seventeenth day of the month, on that day all the sources of the vast watery depths burst open, the floodgates of the sky were opened, [12] and the rain fell on the earth forty days and forty nights. [13] On that same day Noah and his three sons, Shem, Ham, and Japheth, entered the ark, along with Noah's wife and his three sons' wives. [14] They entered it with all the wildlife according to their kinds, all livestock according to their kinds, all the creatures that crawl on the earth according to their kinds, every flying creature—all the birds and every winged creature—according to their kinds. [15] Two of every creature that has the breath of life in it came to Noah and entered the ark. [16] Those that entered, male and female of every creature, entered just as God had commanded him. Then the LORD shut him in.

GENESIS 8:1–22

The Flood Recedes

[1] God remembered Noah, as well as all the wildlife and all the livestock that were with him in the ark. God caused a wind to pass over the earth, and the water began to subside. [2] The sources of the watery depths and the floodgates of the sky were closed, and the rain from the sky stopped. [3] The water steadily receded from the earth, and by the end of 150 days the water had decreased significantly. [4] The ark came to rest in the seventh month, on the seventeenth day of the month, on the mountains of Ararat.

[5] The water continued to recede until the tenth month; in the tenth month, on the first day of the month, the tops of the mountains were visible. [6] After forty days Noah opened the window of the ark that he had made, [7] and he sent out a raven. It went back and forth until the water had dried up from the earth. [8] Then he sent out a dove to see whether the water on the earth's surface had gone down, [9] but the dove found no resting place for its foot. It returned to him in the ark because water covered the surface of the whole earth. He reached out and brought it into the ark to himself. [10] So Noah waited seven more days and sent out the dove from the ark again. [11] When the dove came to him at evening, there was a plucked olive leaf in its beak. So Noah knew that the water on the earth's surface had gone down. [12] After he had waited another seven days, he sent out the dove, but it did not return to him again. [13] In the six hundred first year, in the first month, on the first day of the month, the water that had covered the earth was dried up. Then Noah removed the ark's cover and saw that the surface of the ground was drying. [14] By the twenty-seventh day of the second month, the earth was dry.

The Lord's Promise

[15] Then God spoke to Noah, [16] "Come out of the ark, you, your wife, your sons, and your sons' wives with you. [17] Bring out all the living creatures that are with you—birds, livestock, those that crawl on the earth—and they will spread over the earth and be fruitful and multiply on the earth." [18] So Noah, along with his sons, his wife, and his sons' wives, came out. [19] All the animals, all the creatures that crawl, and all the flying creatures—everything that moves on the earth—came out of the ark by their families.

[20] Then Noah built an altar to the LORD. He took some of every kind of clean animal and every kind of clean bird and offered burnt offerings on the altar. [21] When the LORD smelled the pleasing aroma, he said to himself, "I will never again curse the ground because of human beings, even though the inclination of the human heart is evil from youth onward. And I will never again strike down every living thing as I have done.

[22] As long as the earth endures,
seedtime and harvest, cold and heat,
summer and winter, and day and night
will not cease."

GENESIS 9:12–17

[12] And God said, "This is the sign of the covenant I am making between me and you and every living creature with you, a covenant for all future generations: [13] I have placed my bow in the clouds, and it will be a sign of the covenant between me and the earth. [14] Whenever I form clouds over the earth and the bow appears in the clouds, [15] I will remember my covenant between me and you and all the living creatures: water will never again become a flood to destroy every creature. [16] The bow will be in the clouds, and I will look at it and remember the permanent covenant between God and all the living creatures on earth." [17] God said to Noah, "This is the sign of the covenant that I have established between me and every creature on earth."

❤ GOING DEEPER

EPHESIANS 2:8–9

[8] For you are saved by grace through faith, and this is not from yourselves; it is God's gift— [9] not from works, so that no one can boast.

NOTES / NOTES

REMEMBER  GOD'S RESCUE

EXODUS 2:23–25

²³ After a long time, the king of Egypt died. The Israelites groaned because of their difficult labor, they cried out, and their cry for help because of the difficult labor ascended to God.

²⁴ God heard their groaning, and God remembered his covenant with Abraham, with Isaac, and with Jacob.

²⁵ God saw the Israelites, and God knew.

EXODUS 6:2–8

God Promises Freedom

² Then God spoke to Moses, telling him, "I am the Lord. ³ I appeared to Abraham, Isaac, and Jacob as God Almighty, but I was not known to them by my name 'the Lord.' ⁴ I also established my covenant with them to give them the land of Canaan, the land they lived in as aliens. ⁵ Furthermore, I have heard the groaning of the Israelites, whom the Egyptians are forcing to work as slaves, and I have remembered my covenant.

⁶ "Therefore tell the Israelites: I am the Lord, and I will bring you out from the forced labor of the Egyptians and rescue you from slavery to them. I will redeem you with an outstretched arm and great acts of judgment. ⁷ I will take you as my people, and I will be your God. You will know that I am the Lord your God, who brought you out from the forced labor of the Egyptians. ⁸ I will bring you to the land that I swore to give to Abraham, Isaac, and Jacob, and I will give it to you as a possession. I am the Lord."

EXODUS 12:1–42

Instructions for the Passover

¹ The Lord said to Moses and Aaron in the land of Egypt, ² "This month is to be the beginning of months for you; it is the first month of your year. ³ Tell the whole community of Israel that on the tenth day of this month they must each select an animal of the flock according to their fathers' families, one animal per family. ⁴ If the household is too small for a whole animal, that person and the neighbor nearest his house are to select one based on the combined number of people; you should apportion the animal according to what each will eat. ⁵ You must have an unblemished animal, a year-old male; you may take it from either the sheep or the goats. ⁶ You are to keep it until the fourteenth day of this month; then the whole assembly of the community of Israel will slaughter the animals at twilight. ⁷ They must take some of the blood and put it on the two doorposts and the lintel of the houses where they eat them. ⁸ They are to eat the meat that night; they should eat it, roasted over the fire along with unleavened bread and bitter herbs. ⁹ Do not eat any of it raw or cooked in boiling water, but only roasted over fire—its head as well as its legs and inner organs. ¹⁰ You must not leave any of it until morning; any part of it left until morning you must burn. ¹¹ Here is how you must eat

it: You must be dressed for travel, your sandals on your feet, and your staff in your hand. You are to eat it in a hurry; it is the LORD's Passover.

¹² "I will pass through the land of Egypt on that night and strike every firstborn male in the land of Egypt, both people and animals. I am the LORD; I will execute judgments against all the gods of Egypt. ¹³ The blood on the houses where you are staying will be a distinguishing mark for you; when I see the blood, I will pass over you. No plague will be among you to destroy you when I strike the land of Egypt.

¹⁴ "This day is to be a memorial for you, and you must celebrate it as a festival to the LORD. You are to celebrate it throughout your generations as a permanent statute. ¹⁵ You must eat unleavened bread for seven days. On the first day you must remove yeast from your houses. Whoever eats what is leavened from the first day through the seventh day must be cut off from Israel. ¹⁶ You are to hold a sacred assembly on the first day and another sacred assembly on the seventh day. No work may be done on those days except for preparing what people need to eat—you may do only that.

¹⁷ "You are to observe the Festival of Unleavened Bread because on this very day I brought your military divisions out of the land of Egypt. You must observe this day throughout your generations as a permanent statute. ¹⁸ You are to eat unleavened bread in the first month, from the evening of the fourteenth day of the month until the evening of the twenty-first day. ¹⁹ Yeast must not be found in your houses for seven days. If anyone eats something leavened, that person, whether a resident alien or native of the land, must be cut off from the community of Israel. ²⁰ Do not eat anything leavened; eat unleavened bread in all your homes."

²¹ Then Moses summoned all the elders of Israel and said to them, "Go, select an animal from the flock according to your families, and slaughter the Passover animal. ²² Take a cluster of hyssop, dip it in the blood that is in the basin, and brush the lintel and the two doorposts with some of the blood in the basin. None of you may go out the door of his house until morning. ²³ When the LORD passes through to strike

Egypt and sees the blood on the lintel and the two doorposts, he will pass over the door and not let the destroyer enter your houses to strike you.

24 "Keep this command permanently as a statute for you and your descendants. 25 When you enter the land that the LORD will give you as he promised, you are to observe this ceremony. 26 When your children ask you, 'What does this ceremony mean to you?' 27 you are to reply, 'It is the Passover sacrifice to the LORD, for he passed over the houses of the Israelites in Egypt when he struck the Egyptians, and he spared our homes.'" So the people knelt low and worshiped. 28 Then the Israelites went and did this; they did just as the LORD had commanded Moses and Aaron.

The Exodus

29 Now at midnight the LORD struck every firstborn male in the land of Egypt, from the firstborn of Pharaoh who sat on his throne to the firstborn of the prisoner who was in the dungeon, and every firstborn of the livestock. 30 During the night Pharaoh got up, he along with all his officials and all the Egyptians, and there was a loud wailing throughout Egypt because there wasn't a house without someone dead. 31 He summoned Moses and Aaron during the night and said, "Get out immediately from among my people, both you and the Israelites, and go, worship the LORD as you have said. 32 Take even your flocks and your herds as you asked and leave, and also bless me."

33 Now the Egyptians pressured the people in order to send them quickly out of the country, for they said, "We're all going to die!" 34 So the people took their dough before it was leavened, with their kneading bowls wrapped up in their clothes on their shoulders.

35 The Israelites acted on Moses's word and asked the Egyptians for silver and gold items and for clothing. 36 And the LORD gave the people such favor with the Egyptians that they gave them what they requested. In this way they plundered the Egyptians.

37 The Israelites traveled from Rameses to Succoth, about six hundred thousand able-bodied men on foot, besides their families. 38 A mixed crowd also went up with them, along with a huge number of livestock, both flocks and herds. 39 The people baked the dough they had brought out of Egypt into unleavened loaves, since it had no yeast; for when they were driven out of Egypt, they could not delay and had not prepared provisions for themselves.

40 The time that the Israelites lived in Egypt was 430 years. 41 At the end of 430 years, on that same day, all the LORD's military divisions went out from the land of Egypt. 42 It was a night of vigil in honor of the LORD, because he would bring them out of the land of Egypt. This same night is in honor of the LORD, a night vigil for all the Israelites throughout their generations.

EXODUS 13:3–16

3 Then Moses said to the people, "Remember this day when you came out of Egypt, out of the place of slavery, for the LORD brought you out of here by the strength of his hand. Nothing leavened may be eaten. 4 Today, in the month of Abib, you are going out. 5 When the LORD brings you into the land of the Canaanites, Hethites, Amorites, Hivites, and Jebusites, which he swore to your ancestors that he would give you, a land flowing with milk and honey, you must carry out this ceremony in this month. 6 For seven days you must eat unleavened bread, and on the seventh day there is to be a festival to the LORD. 7 Unleavened bread is to be eaten for those seven days. Nothing leavened may be found among you, and no yeast may be found among you in all your territory. 8 On that day explain to your son, 'This is because of what the LORD did for me when I came out of Egypt.'

9 Let it serve as a sign for you on your hand and as a reminder on your forehead,

so that the LORD's instruction may be in your mouth; for the LORD brought you out of Egypt with a strong hand. 10 Keep this statute at its appointed time from year to year.

11 "When the LORD brings you into the land of the Canaanites, as he swore to you and your ancestors, and gives it to you, 12 you are to present to the LORD every firstborn male of the womb. All firstborn offspring of the livestock you

own that are males will be the Lord's. [13] You must redeem every firstborn of a donkey with a flock animal, but if you do not redeem it, break its neck. However, you must redeem every firstborn among your sons.

[14] "In the future, when your son asks you, 'What does this mean?' say to him, 'By the strength of his hand the Lord brought us out of Egypt, out of the place of slavery. [15] When Pharaoh stubbornly refused to let us go, the Lord killed every firstborn male in the land of Egypt, both the firstborn of humans and the firstborn of livestock. That is why I sacrifice to the Lord all the firstborn of the womb that are males, but I redeem all the firstborn of my sons.' [16] So let it be a sign on your hand and a symbol on your forehead, for the Lord brought us out of Egypt by the strength of his hand."

♥ GOING DEEPER

JOHN 1:29–30

The Lamb of God

[29] The next day John saw Jesus coming toward him and said, "Look, the Lamb of God, who takes away the sin of the world! [30] This is the one I told you about: 'After me comes a man who ranks ahead of me, because he existed before me.'"

REMEMBER GOD'S PROVISION

For the LORD your God dried up the water of the Jordan before you until you had crossed over...

JOSHUA 4:23

JOSHUA 1:1–5, 10–11

Encouragement of Joshua

¹ After the death of Moses the LORD's servant, the LORD spoke to Joshua son of Nun, Moses's assistant: ² "Moses my servant is dead. Now you and all the people prepare to cross over the Jordan to the land I am giving the Israelites. ³ I have given you every place where the sole of your foot treads, just as I promised Moses. ⁴ Your territory will be from the wilderness and Lebanon to the great river, the Euphrates River—all the land of the Hittites—and west to the Mediterranean Sea. ⁵ No one will be able to stand against you as long as you live. I will be with you, just as I was with Moses. I will not leave you or abandon you."

…

Joshua Prepares the People

¹⁰ Then Joshua commanded the officers of the people, ¹¹ "Go through the camp and tell the people, 'Get provisions ready for yourselves, for within three days you will be crossing the Jordan to go in and take possession of the land the LORD your God is giving you to inherit.'"

JOSHUA 3:5–17

⁵ Joshua told the people, "Consecrate yourselves, because the LORD will do wonders among you tomorrow." ⁶ Then he said to the priests, "Carry the ark of the covenant and go on ahead of the people." So they carried the ark of the covenant and went ahead of them.

⁷ The LORD spoke to Joshua: "Today I will begin to exalt you in the sight of all Israel, so they will know that I will be with you just as I was with Moses. ⁸ Command the priests carrying the ark of the covenant: When you reach the edge of the water, stand in the Jordan."

⁹ Then Joshua told the Israelites, "Come closer and listen to the words of the LORD your God." ¹⁰ He said, "You will know that the living God is among you and that he will certainly dispossess before you the Canaanites, Hethites, Hivites, Perizzites, Girgashites, Amorites, and Jebusites ¹¹ when the ark of the covenant of the Lord of the whole earth goes ahead of you into the Jordan. ¹² Now choose twelve men from the tribes of Israel, one man for each tribe. ¹³ When the feet of the priests who carry the ark of the LORD, the Lord of the whole earth, come to rest in the Jordan's water, its water will be cut off. The water flowing downstream will stand up in a mass."

[14] When the people broke camp to cross the Jordan, the priests carried the ark of the covenant ahead of the people. [15] Now the Jordan overflows its banks throughout the harvest season. But as soon as the priests carrying the ark reached the Jordan, their feet touched the water at its edge [16] and the water flowing downstream stood still, rising up in a mass that extended as far as Adam, a city next to Zarethan. The water flowing downstream into the Sea of the Arabah—the Dead Sea—was completely cut off, and the people crossed opposite Jericho. [17] The priests carrying the ark of the LORD's covenant stood firmly on dry ground in the middle of the Jordan, while all Israel crossed on dry ground until the entire nation had finished crossing the Jordan.

Flip to page 82 to see other examples of remembrance throughout the Old and New Testaments.

JOSHUA 4
The Memorial Stones

[1] After the entire nation had finished crossing the Jordan, the LORD spoke to Joshua: [2] "Choose twelve men from the people, one man for each tribe, [3] and command them: Take twelve stones from this place in the middle of the Jordan where the priests are standing, carry them with you, and set them down at the place where you spend the night."

[4] So Joshua summoned the twelve men he had selected from the Israelites, one man for each tribe, [5] and said to them, "Go across to the ark of the LORD your God in the middle of the Jordan. Each of you lift a stone onto his shoulder, one for each of the Israelite tribes, [6] so that this will be a sign among you. In the future, when your children ask you, 'What do these stones mean to you?' [7] you should tell them, 'The water of the Jordan was cut off in front of the ark of the LORD's covenant. When it crossed the Jordan, the Jordan's water was cut off.'

Therefore these stones will always be a memorial for the Israelites."

[8] The Israelites did just as Joshua had commanded them. The twelve men took stones from the middle of the Jordan, one for each of the Israelite tribes, just as the LORD had told Joshua. They carried them to the camp and set them down there. [9] Joshua also set up twelve stones in the middle of the Jordan where the priests who carried the ark of the covenant were standing. The stones are still there today.

¹⁰ The priests carrying the ark continued standing in the middle of the Jordan until everything was completed that the LORD had commanded Joshua to tell the people, in keeping with all that Moses had commanded Joshua. The people hurried across, ¹¹ and after everyone had finished crossing, the priests with the ark of the LORD crossed in the sight of the people. ¹² The Reubenites, Gadites, and half the tribe of Manasseh went in battle formation in front of the Israelites, as Moses had instructed them. ¹³ About forty thousand equipped for war crossed to the plains of Jericho in the LORD's presence.

¹⁴ On that day the LORD exalted Joshua in the sight of all Israel, and they revered him throughout his life, as they had revered Moses. ¹⁵ The LORD told Joshua, ¹⁶ "Command the priests who carry the ark of the testimony to come up from the Jordan."

¹⁷ So Joshua commanded the priests, "Come up from the Jordan." ¹⁸ When the priests carrying the ark of the LORD's covenant came up from the middle of the Jordan, and their feet stepped out on solid ground, the water of the Jordan resumed its course, flowing over all the banks as before.

¹⁹ The people came up from the Jordan on the tenth day of the first month, and camped at Gilgal on the eastern limits of Jericho. ²⁰ Then Joshua set up in Gilgal the twelve stones they had taken from the Jordan, ²¹ and he said to the Israelites, "In the future, when your children ask their fathers, 'What is the meaning of these stones?' ²² you should tell your children, 'Israel crossed the Jordan on dry ground.' ²³ For the LORD your God dried up the water of the Jordan before you until you had crossed over, just as the LORD your God did to the Red Sea, which he dried up before us until we had crossed over. ²⁴ This is so that all the peoples of the earth may know that the LORD's hand is strong, and so that you may always fear the LORD your God."

♥ GOING DEEPER

PSALM 16:5–6

⁵ LORD, you are my portion
and my cup of blessing;
you hold my future.
⁶ The boundary lines have fallen for me
in pleasant places;
indeed, I have a beautiful inheritance.

LUKE 1:68

Blessed is the Lord, the God of Israel,
because he has visited
and provided redemption for his people.

ROMANS 8:28

We know that all things work together for the good of those who love God, who are called according to his purpose.

REMEMBER GOD'S WORD AND WAYS

DAY 05

These words that I am giving you today are to be in your heart. Repeat them to your children. Talk about them when you sit in your house and when you walk along the road, when you lie down and when you get up.

DEUTERONOMY 6:6–7

DEUTERONOMY 6:4–25

[4] Listen, Israel: The LORD our God, the LORD is one. [5] Love the LORD your God with all your heart, with all your soul, and with all your strength. [6] These words that I am giving you today are to be in your heart. [7] Repeat them to your children. Talk about them when you sit in your house and when you walk along the road, when you lie down and when you get up. [8] Bind them as a sign on your hand and let them be a symbol on your forehead. [9] Write them on the doorposts of your house and on your city gates.

Remembering God Through Obedience

[10] When the LORD your God brings you into the land he swore to your ancestors Abraham, Isaac, and Jacob that he would give you—a land with large and beautiful cities that you did not build, [11] houses full of every good thing that you did not fill them with, cisterns that you did not dig, and vineyards and olive groves that you did not plant—and when you eat and are satisfied, [12] be careful not to forget the LORD who brought you out of the land of Egypt, out of the place of slavery. [13] Fear the LORD your God, worship him, and take your oaths in his name. [14] Do not follow other gods, the gods of the peoples around you, [15] for the LORD your God, who is among you, is a jealous God. Otherwise, the LORD your God will become angry with you and obliterate you from the face of the earth. [16] Do not test the LORD your God as you tested him at Massah. [17] Carefully observe the commands of the LORD your God, the decrees and statutes he has commanded you. [18] Do what is right and good in the LORD's sight, so that you may prosper and so that you may enter and possess the good land the LORD your God swore to give your ancestors, [19] by driving out all your enemies before you, as the LORD has said.

[20] When your son asks you in the future, "What is the meaning of the decrees, statutes, and ordinances that the LORD our God has commanded you?" [21] tell him, "We were slaves of Pharaoh in Egypt, but the LORD brought us out of Egypt with a strong hand. [22] Before our eyes the LORD inflicted great and devastating signs and wonders on Egypt, on Pharaoh, and on all his household, [23] but he brought us from there in order to lead us in and give us the land that he swore to our ancestors. [24] The LORD commanded us to follow all these statutes and to fear the LORD our God for our prosperity always and for our preservation, as it is today. [25] Righteousness will be ours if we are careful to follow every one of these commands before the LORD our God, as he has commanded us."

NUMBERS 15:37–41

Tassels for Remembrance

[37] The LORD said to Moses, [38] "Speak to the Israelites and tell them that throughout their generations they are to make tassels for the corners of their garments, and put a blue cord on the tassel at each corner. [39] These will serve as tassels for you to look at, so that you may remember all the LORD's commands and obey them and not prostitute yourselves by following your own heart and your own eyes. [40] This way you will remember and obey all my commands and be holy to your God. [41] I am the LORD your God who brought you out of the land of Egypt to be your God; I am the LORD your God."

PSALM 119:16

I will delight in your statutes;
I will not forget your word.

PSALM 77:11–12

[11] I will remember the LORD's works;
yes, I will remember your ancient wonders.
[12] I will reflect on all you have done
and meditate on your actions.

🔖 GOING DEEPER

2 PETER 1:3–15

Growth in the Faith

[3] His divine power has given us everything required for life and godliness through the knowledge of him who called us by his own glory and goodness. [4] By these he has given us very great and precious promises, so that through them you may share in the divine nature, escaping the corruption that

is in the world because of evil desire. [5] For this very reason, make every effort to supplement your faith with goodness, goodness with knowledge, [6] knowledge with self-control, self-control with endurance, endurance with godliness, [7] godliness with brotherly affection, and brotherly affection with love. [8] For if you possess these qualities in increasing measure, they will keep you from being useless or unfruitful in the knowledge of our Lord Jesus Christ. [9] The person who lacks these things is blind and shortsighted and has forgotten the cleansing from his past sins. [10] Therefore, brothers and sisters, make every effort to confirm your calling and election, because if you do these things you will never stumble. [11] For in this way, entry into the eternal kingdom of our Lord and Savior Jesus Christ will be richly provided for you.

[12] Therefore I will always remind you about these things, even though you know them and are established in the truth you now have. [13] I think it is right, as long as I am in this bodily tent, to wake you up with a reminder,

[14] since I know that I will soon lay aside my tent, as our Lord Jesus Christ has indeed made clear to me. [15] And I will also make every effort so that you are able to recall these things at any time after my departure.

PRACTICING REMEMBRANCE

Because biblical remembrance is both mental and physical, we practice remembrance when we pair our reflections and introspections with tangible acts that serve as reminders of truth.

The following is a framework for how we can build and practice the spiritual discipline of remembering in our daily lives.

Each week, you will have the opportunity to reflect on what you've read and to make a plan for how you want to respond with a particular method of remembrance.

KNOW THE STORY

As believers, the practice of reading and meditating on God's Word focuses our attention on His truth and His larger story of redemption. This is what we do each time we read and engage as women in the Word of God every day!

You can practice memorizing Scripture (that's why Sundays are set aside for Scripture memorization!), so that you can draw on His truth in your daily life.

WRITE DOWN YOUR STORY

Writing the stories of God's movement in our lives gives a clear picture to return to if and when we encounter a similar experience later. Often, it's in recording our stories that we pay attention to the ways we have seen God at work that we didn't notice before.

If you don't already, try recording the significant moments in your faith where you encountered God's presence and goodness, or saw His promises fulfilled in your life. Think about what's been hard and where you've seen God provide. How did you feel, what were your fears, and who was with you during that time? Where did you experience God? If you already do this, return to your journals or records and reflect on what you wrote.

SHARE STORIES IN COMMUNITY

Before the individual books of the Bible were put together into one complete book, God's people passed stories of His wisdom, works, and wonders through oral tradition. This oral tradition preserved histories and teachings so future generations could remember God's work among His people. Like the forerunners of our faith, we need the stories of our fellow believers to encourage us to persevere and walk in obedience to God.

The time you spend and the conversations you have with your community are how you can practice remembrance as a member of the body of Christ. Whether you are building relationships with people you don't know or deepening ties with friends who are already close, ask to hear about what God has done and is doing in the lives of the people around you. And even when vulnerability is hard, share your stories in response.

MARK A MILESTONE

In Scripture we see several examples of God calling His people to establish reminders of His faithfulness (see "Markers of Remembrance in Scripture" on page 82). Sometimes it's an object, a physical marker, or special celebration.

You can mirror the examples in these stories when you engage with acts of remembrance that are already built into the spiritual rhythms of the Church. You can participate in communion, celebrate baptisms, or serve in your local church community. Think about how you can be a part of marking important dates for the Christian community (such as Easter and Christmas). You can also celebrate and note moments that are significant in your personal faith story, like the anniversary of your salvation, baptism, serving with a ministry, or a difficult season where God provided.

RESPONSE / RESPONSE

Remembering is active, both in how we think and in how we respond with our actions. Each day's reading title, listed below, reminds us of a specific aspect of God's character that we are prone to forget. Use this space to make a plan for how you want to act on God's truth through practicing remembrance over the next week.

REMEMBER GOD'S <u>PROMISES</u>

REMEMBER GOD'S <u>MERCY</u>

REMEMBER GOD'S <u>RESCUE</u>

REMEMBER GOD'S <u>PROVISION</u>

REMEMBER GOD'S <u>WORD AND WAYS</u>

Take some time to reflect on each of these aspects that you read about this week. Which one are you most prone to forget? Write it in the space provided below.

With what you are most prone to forget as a guide, use this space to plan how you will practice remembrance this week.

First, choose from one of the following methods. Or come up with your own! Then, using the following questions, plan how you will practice this specific method in the coming week.

⬭ KNOW THE STORY

⬭ WRITE DOWN YOUR STORY

⬭ SHARE STORIES IN COMMUNITY

⬭ MARK A MILESTONE

⬭ OTHER: _____

How will I do this?

When will I do this?

Who can I invite into this process with me?

GRACE DAY

REMEMBER HIS
COVENANT
FOREVER—THE
PROMISE HE
ORDAINED FOR
A THOUSAND
GENERATIONS.

1 CHRONICLES 16:15

WEEK ONE / DAY SIX

Take this day to catch up on
your reading, pray, and rest
in the presence of the Lord.

DAY

07

DAY

Scripture is God-breathed and true. When we memorize it, we carry the good news of Jesus with us wherever we go.

Throughout this plan, one of the ways we will practice remembrance is by committing our key passage to memory. We will use different Scripture memorization tools to fill our hearts and minds with the truth of God's Word.

Read the passage out loud several times. Circle or highlight the words that stand out to you. Then read the passage again, emphasizing each word you noted.

I WILL REMEMBER THE LORD'S WORKS; YES, I WILL REMEMBER YOUR ANCIENT WONDERS. I WILL REFLECT ON ALL YOU HAVE DONE AND MEDITATE ON YOUR ACTIONS.

PSALM 77:11–12

See additional tips for memorizing Scripture on page 100.

GOD

WEEK

02

REMEMBERS US

God is unwaveringly faithful. Because of this, we can cry out for Him to remember us: for Him to act in the present according to what we know is true of His proven character. In seasons of trial, uncertainty, need, and everything in between, Scripture demonstrates God is faithful to provide and forgive our sins and shortcomings. He does not forget His people.

In this week's readings, we will join the voices of psalmists, prophets, and other followers of God who call on Him to remember and meet their specific needs.

"LOOK, I HAVE INSCRIBED YOU ON THE PALMS OF MY HANDS..."

ISAIAH 49:16

GOD, REMEMBER YOUR PEOPLE

ISAIAH 49:14–18

Zion Remembered

14 Zion says, "The Lord has abandoned me;
the Lord has forgotten me!"

15 "Can a woman forget her nursing child,
or lack compassion for the child of her womb?
Even if these forget,
yet I will not forget you.

16 Look, I have inscribed you on the palms of my hands;
your walls are continually before me.

17 Your builders hurry;
those who destroy and devastate you will leave you.

18 Look up, and look around.
They all gather together; they come to you.
As I live"—
this is the Lord's declaration—
"you will wear all your children as jewelry,
and put them on as a bride does."

JEREMIAH 31:7–14, 16–25

God's People Brought Home

7 For this is what the Lord says:

Sing with joy for Jacob;
shout for the foremost of the nations!
Proclaim, praise, and say,
"Lord, save your people,
the remnant of Israel!"

8 Watch! I am going to bring them from the
northern land.
I will gather them from remote regions of the earth—
the blind and the lame will be with them,
along with those who are pregnant and those about
to give birth.
They will return here as a great assembly!

9 They will come weeping,
but I will bring them back with consolation.

I will lead them to wadis filled with water,
by a smooth way where they will not stumble,
for I am Israel's Father,
and Ephraim is my firstborn.
¹⁰ Nations, hear the word of the Lord,
and tell it among the far off coasts and islands!
Say, "The one who scattered Israel will gather him.
He will watch over him as a shepherd guards his flock,
¹¹ for the Lord has ransomed Jacob
and redeemed him from the power of one stronger
    than he."
¹² They will come and shout for joy on the heights of Zion;

they will be radiant with joy

because of the Lord's goodness,

because of the grain, the new wine, the fresh oil,
and because of the young of the flocks and herds.
Their life will be like an irrigated garden,
and they will no longer grow weak from hunger.
¹³ Then the young women will rejoice with dancing,
while young and old men rejoice together.
I will turn their mourning into joy,
give them consolation,
and bring happiness out of grief.
¹⁴ I will refresh the priests with an abundance,
and my people will be satisfied with my goodness.
    This is the Lord's declaration.

. . .

¹⁶ This is what the Lord says:

Keep your voice from weeping
and your eyes from tears,
for the reward for your work will come—
    this is the Lord's declaration—
and your children will return from the enemy's land.
¹⁷ There is hope for your future—
    this is the Lord's declaration—
and your children will return to their own territory.
¹⁸ I have surely heard Ephraim moaning,
"You disciplined me, and I have been disciplined
like an untrained calf.
Take me back, so that I can return,

for you, Lord, are my God.
¹⁹ After my return, I felt regret;
After I was instructed, I struck my thigh in grief.
I was ashamed and humiliated
because I bore the disgrace of my youth."
²⁰ Isn't Ephraim a precious son to me,
a delightful child?
Whenever I speak against him,
I certainly still think about him.
Therefore, my inner being yearns for him;
I will truly have compassion on him.
    This is the Lord's declaration.

Repentance and Restoration
²¹ Set up road markers for yourself;
establish signposts!
Keep the highway in mind,
the way you have traveled.
Return, Virgin Israel!
Return to these cities of yours.
²² How long will you turn here and there,
faithless daughter?
For the Lord creates something new in the land—
a female will shelter a man.

²³ This is what the Lord of Armies, the God of Israel, says: "When I restore their fortunes, they will once again speak this word in the land of Judah and in its cities: 'May the Lord bless you, righteous settlement, holy mountain.' ²⁴ Judah and all its cities will live in it together—also farmers and those who move with the flocks— ²⁵ for I satisfy the thirsty person and feed all those who are weak."

◆ **GOING DEEPER**

1 PETER 2:9–10
⁹ But you are a chosen race, a royal priesthood, a holy nation, a people for his possession, so that you may proclaim the praises of the one who called you out of darkness into his marvelous light. ¹⁰ Once you were not a people, but now you are God's people; you had not received mercy, but now you have received mercy.

NOTES / NOTES

GOD, REMEMBER OUR SUFFERING

PSALM 74:1–2

Prayer for Israel
A Maskil *of Asaph.*

¹ Why have you rejected us forever, God?
Why does your anger burn
against the sheep of your pasture?
² Remember your congregation,
which you purchased long ago
and redeemed as the tribe for your own possession.
Remember Mount Zion where you dwell.

JEREMIAH 15:15–18

Jeremiah's Prayer for Vengeance

¹⁵ You know, LORD;

remember me and take note of me.

Avenge me against my persecutors.
In your patience, don't take me away.
Know that I suffer disgrace for your honor.
¹⁶ Your words were found, and I ate them.
Your words became a delight to me
and the joy of my heart,
for I bear your name,
LORD God of Armies.
¹⁷ I never sat with the band of revelers,
and I did not celebrate with them.

Because your hand was on me, I sat alone,
for you filled me with indignation.
¹⁸ Why has my pain become unending,
my wound incurable,
refusing to be healed?
You truly have become like a mirage to me—
water that is not reliable.

PSALM 143

A Cry for Help
A psalm of David.

¹ LORD, hear my prayer.
In your faithfulness listen to my plea,
and in your righteousness answer me.
² Do not bring your servant into judgment,
for no one alive is righteous in your sight.

³ For the enemy has pursued me,
crushing me to the ground,
making me live in darkness
like those long dead.
⁴ My spirit is weak within me;
my heart is overcome with dismay.

[5] I remember the days of old;
I meditate on all you have done;
I reflect on the work of your hands.
[6] I spread out my hands to you;
I am like parched land before you.   *Selah*

[7] Answer me quickly, LORD;
my spirit fails.
Don't hide your face from me,
or I will be like those
going down to the Pit.
[8] Let me experience
your faithful love in the morning,
for I trust in you.
Reveal to me the way I should go
because I appeal to you.
[9] Rescue me from my enemies, LORD;
I come to you for protection.
[10] Teach me to do your will,
for you are my God.
May your gracious Spirit
lead me on level ground.

[11] For your name's sake, LORD,
let me live.
In your righteousness deliver me from trouble,
[12] and in your faithful love destroy my enemies.
Wipe out all those who attack me,
for I am your servant.

⬥ GOING DEEPER

2 CORINTHIANS 1:3–7
The God of Comfort

[3] Blessed be the God and Father of our Lord Jesus Christ, the Father of mercies and the God of all comfort. [4] He comforts us in all our affliction, so that we may be able to comfort those who are in any kind of affliction, through the comfort we ourselves receive from God. [5] For just as the sufferings of Christ overflow to us, so also through Christ our comfort overflows. [6] If we are afflicted, it is for your comfort and salvation. If we are comforted, it is for your comfort, which produces in you patient endurance of the same sufferings that we suffer. [7] And our hope for you is firm, because we know that as you share in the sufferings, so you will also share in the comfort.

GOD, REMEMBER OUR FUTURE

Lᴏʀᴅ of Armies, if you will take notice of your servant's affliction, remember and not forget me, and give your servant a son, I will give him to the Lᴏʀᴅ...

1 SAMUEL 1:11

1 SAMUEL 1:1–20

Hannah's Vow

¹ There was a man from Ramathaim-zophim in the hill country of Ephraim. His name was Elkanah son of Jeroham, son of Elihu, son of Tohu, son of Zuph, an Ephraimite. ² He had two wives, the first named Hannah and the second Peninnah. Peninnah had children, but Hannah was childless. ³ This man would go up from his town every year to worship and to sacrifice to the LORD of Armies at Shiloh, where Eli's two sons, Hophni and Phinehas, were the LORD's priests.

⁴ Whenever Elkanah offered a sacrifice, he always gave portions of the meat to his wife Peninnah and to each of her sons and daughters. ⁵ But he gave a double portion to Hannah, for he loved her even though the LORD had kept her from conceiving. ⁶ Her rival would taunt her severely just to provoke her, because the LORD had kept Hannah from conceiving. ⁷ Year after year, when she went up to the LORD's house, her rival taunted her in this way. Hannah would weep and would not eat. ⁸ "Hannah, why are you crying?" her husband, Elkanah, would ask. "Why won't you eat? Why are you troubled? Am I not better to you than ten sons?"

⁹ On one occasion, Hannah got up after they ate and drank at Shiloh. The priest Eli was sitting on a chair by the doorpost of the LORD's temple. ¹⁰ Deeply hurt, Hannah prayed to the LORD and wept with many tears. ¹¹ Making a vow, she pleaded, "LORD of Armies, if you will take notice of your servant's affliction, remember and not forget me, and give your servant a son, I will give him to the LORD all the days of his life, and his hair will never be cut."

¹² While she continued praying in the LORD's presence, Eli watched her mouth. ¹³ Hannah was praying silently, and though her lips were moving, her voice could not be heard. Eli thought she was drunk ¹⁴ and said to her, "How long are you going to be drunk? Get rid of your wine!"

¹⁵ "No, my lord," Hannah replied. "I am a woman with a broken heart. I haven't had any wine or beer; I've been pouring out my heart before the LORD. ¹⁶ Don't think of me as a wicked woman; I've been praying from the depth of my anguish and resentment."

¹⁷ Eli responded, "Go in peace, and may the God of Israel grant the request you've made of him."

[18] "May your servant find favor with you," she replied. Then Hannah went on her way; she ate and no longer looked despondent.

Samuel's Birth and Dedication

[19] The next morning Elkanah and Hannah got up early to worship before the LORD. Afterward, they returned home to Ramah. Then Elkanah was intimate with his wife Hannah, and the LORD remembered her. [20] After some time, Hannah conceived and gave birth to a son. She named him Samuel, because she said, "I requested him from the LORD."

PSALM 139:7–16

[7] Where can I go to escape your Spirit?
Where can I flee from your presence?
[8] If I go up to heaven, you are there;
if I make my bed in Sheol, you are there.
[9] If I fly on the wings of the dawn
and settle down on the western horizon,
[10] even there your hand will lead me;
your right hand will hold on to me.
[11] If I say, "Surely the darkness will hide me,
and the light around me will be night"—
[12] even the darkness is not dark to you.
The night shines like the day;
darkness and light are alike to you.

[13] For it was you who created my inward parts;
you knit me together in my mother's womb.
[14] I will praise you
because I have been remarkably and wondrously made.
Your works are wondrous,
and I know this very well.
[15] My bones were not hidden from you
when I was made in secret,
when I was formed in the depths of the earth.
[16] Your eyes saw me when I was formless;

all my days were written in your book

   and planned

before a single one of them began.

MATTHEW 26:6–13
The Anointing at Bethany

[6] While Jesus was in Bethany at the house of Simon the leper, [7] a woman approached him with an alabaster jar of very expensive perfume. She poured it on his head as he was reclining at the table. [8] When the disciples saw it, they were indignant. "Why this waste?" they asked. [9] "This might have been sold for a great deal and given to the poor."

[10] Aware of this, Jesus said to them, "Why are you bothering this woman? She has done a noble thing for me. [11] You always have the poor with you, but you do not always have me. [12] By pouring this perfume on my body, she has prepared me for burial. [13] Truly I tell you, wherever this gospel is proclaimed in the whole world, what she has done will also be told in memory of her."

LUKE 23:35–43

[35] The people stood watching, and even the leaders were scoffing: "He saved others; let him save himself if this is God's Messiah, the Chosen One!" [36] The soldiers also mocked him. They came offering him sour wine [37] and said, "If you are the king of the Jews, save yourself!"

[38] An inscription was above him: THIS IS THE KING OF THE JEWS.

[39] Then one of the criminals hanging there began to yell insults at him: "Aren't you the Messiah? Save yourself and us!"

[40] But the other answered, rebuking him: "Don't you even fear God, since you are undergoing the same punishment? [41] We are punished justly, because we're getting back what we deserve for the things we did, but this man has done nothing wrong." [42] Then he said, "Jesus, remember me when you come into your kingdom."

[43] And he said to him, "Truly I tell you, today you will be with me in paradise."

NOTES / NOTES

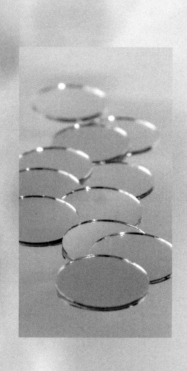

GOD, REMEMBER OUR NEED

DAY 11

I say, "The LORD is my portion, therefore I will put my hope in him."

LAMENTATIONS 3:24

PSALM 23

The Good Shepherd
A psalm of David.

¹ The LORD is my shepherd;
I have what I need.
² He lets me lie down in green pastures;
he leads me beside quiet waters.
³ He renews my life;
he leads me along the right paths
for his name's sake.
⁴ Even when I go through the darkest valley,
I fear no danger,
for you are with me;
your rod and your staff—they comfort me.

⁵ You prepare a table before me
in the presence of my enemies;
you anoint my head with oil;
my cup overflows.
⁶ Only goodness and faithful love will pursue me
all the days of my life,
and I will dwell in the house of the LORD
as long as I live.

LAMENTATIONS 3:19–25, 55–59

ז Zayin
¹⁹ Remember my affliction and my homelessness,
the wormwood and the poison.
²⁰ I continually remember them
and have become depressed.
²¹ Yet I call this to mind,
and therefore I have hope:

ח Cheth
²² Because of the LORD's faithful love
we do not perish,
for his mercies never end.
²³ They are new every morning;
great is your faithfulness!
²⁴ I say, "The LORD is my portion,
therefore I will put my hope in him."

ט Teth
²⁵ The LORD is good to those who wait for him,
to the person who seeks him.

. . .

ק Qoph
⁵⁵ I called on your name, LORD,
from the depths of the pit.
⁵⁶ You heard my plea:
Do not ignore my cry for relief.
⁵⁷ You came near whenever I called you;
you said, "Do not be afraid."

ר Resh

⁵⁸ **You championed my cause, Lord;
you redeemed my life.**

⁵⁹ LORD, you saw the wrong done to me;
judge my case.

◆ GOING DEEPER

LUKE 11:3–4

³ "Give us each day our daily bread.
⁴ And forgive us our sins,
for we ourselves also forgive everyone
in debt to us.
And do not bring us into temptation."

MATTHEW 6:25–33

²⁵ "Therefore I tell you: Don't worry about your life, what you will eat or what you will drink; or about your body, what you will wear. Isn't life more than food and the body more than clothing? ²⁶ Consider the birds of the sky: They don't sow or reap or gather into barns, yet your heavenly Father feeds them. Aren't you worth more than they? ²⁷ Can any of you add one moment to his life span by worrying? ²⁸ And why do you worry about clothes? Observe how the wildflowers of the field grow: They don't labor or spin thread. ²⁹ Yet I tell

you that not even Solomon in all his splendor was adorned like one of these. [30] If that's how God clothes the grass of the field, which is here today and thrown into the furnace tomorrow, won't he do much more for you—you of little faith? [31] So don't worry, saying, 'What will we eat?' or 'What will we drink?' or 'What will we wear?' [32] For the Gentiles eagerly seek all these things, and your heavenly Father knows that you need them. [33] But seek first the kingdom of God and his righteousness, and all these things will be provided for you."

DO NOT REMEMBER THE SINS OF MY YOUTH OR MY ACTS OF REBELLION...

PSALM 25:7

GOD, REMEMBER NOT OUR SIN

PSALM 25:6–7

⁶ Remember, Lord, your compassion
and your faithful love,
for they have existed from antiquity.
⁷ Do not remember the sins of my youth
or my acts of rebellion;
in keeping with your faithful love, remember me
because of your goodness, Lord.

PSALM 51:1

Be gracious to me, God,
according to your faithful love;
according to your abundant compassion,
blot out my rebellion.

ISAIAH 43:16–25

¹⁶ This is what the Lord says—
who makes a way in the sea,
and a path through raging water,
¹⁷ who brings out the chariot and horse,
the army and the mighty one together
(they lie down, they do not rise again;
they are extinguished, put out like a wick)—

¹⁸ "Do not remember the past events;
pay no attention to things of old.
¹⁹ Look, I am about to do something new;
even now it is coming. Do you not see it?
Indeed, I will make a way in the wilderness,
rivers in the desert.
²⁰ Wild animals—
jackals and ostriches—will honor me,
because I provide water in the wilderness,
and rivers in the desert,
to give drink to my chosen people.
²¹ The people I formed for myself
will declare my praise.

²² "But, Jacob, you have not called on me,
because, Israel, you have become weary of me.
²³ You have not brought me your sheep for burnt offerings
or honored me with your sacrifices.
I have not burdened you with offerings
or wearied you with incense.
²⁴ You have not bought me aromatic cane with silver,
or satisfied me with the fat of your sacrifices.
But you have burdened me with your sins;
you have wearied me with your iniquities.

²⁵ "I am the one, I sweep away your transgressions

for my own sake

and remember your sins no more."

PSALM 103:11–12

¹¹ For as high as the heavens are above the earth,
so great is his faithful love
toward those who fear him.
¹² As far as the east is from the west,
so far has he removed
our transgressions from us.

◆ GOING DEEPER

HEBREWS 8:7–12

A Superior Covenant

⁷ For if that first covenant had been faultless, there would have been no occasion for a second one. ⁸ But finding fault with his people, he says:

See, the days are coming, says the Lord,
when I will make a new covenant
with the house of Israel
and with the house of Judah—
⁹ not like the covenant
that I made with their ancestors
on the day I took them by the hand
to lead them out of the land of Egypt.
I showed no concern for them, says the Lord,
because they did not continue in my covenant.
¹⁰ For this is the covenant
that I will make with the house of Israel
after those days, says the Lord:
I will put my laws into their minds
and write them on their hearts.
I will be their God,
and they will be my people.
¹¹ And each person will not teach his fellow citizen,
and each his brother or sister, saying, "Know the Lord,"
because they will all know me,
from the least to the greatest of them.
¹² For I will forgive their wrongdoing,
and I will never again remember their sins.

NOTES / NOTES

RESPONSE / RESPONSE

Remembrance is the active practice of letting the past inform our present thoughts, feelings, and actions. Each day this week (listed below) points to something specific we can call on God to remember. Use this space to make a plan for how you will act on God's truth through the practice of remembering this week.

GOD, REMEMBER **YOUR PEOPLE**

GOD, REMEMBER **OUR SUFFERING**

GOD, REMEMBER **OUR FUTURE**

GOD, REMEMBER **OUR NEED**

GOD, REMEMBER **NOT OUR SIN**

Take some time to reflect on each of these aspects that you read about this week. Where do you most need to remember that you are not forgotten? Write it in the space provided below.

Use this space to plan how you will practice remembrance this week.

First, choose from one of the following methods. Or come up with your own! Then, using the following questions, plan how you will practice this specific method in the coming week. Refer back to "Practicing Remembrance" on page 36 if you need a refresher on what building a rhythm of remembrance can look like in your life.

○ KNOW THE STORY

○ WRITE DOWN YOUR STORY

○ SHARE STORIES IN COMMUNITY

○ MARK A MILESTONE

○ OTHER: _____

How will I do this?

When will I do this?

Who can I invite into this process with me?

GRACE DAY

BECAUSE OF THE LORD'S FAITHFUL LOVE WE DO NOT PERISH, FOR HIS MERCIES NEVER END.

LAMENTATIONS 3:22

Take this day to catch up on your reading, pray, and rest in the presence of the Lord.

DAY **14** DAY

Scripture is God-breathed and true. When we memorize it, we carry the good news of Jesus with us wherever we go.

Throughout this plan we are committing our key passage to memory by using different Scripture memorization tools to fill our hearts and minds with the truth of God's Word.

Use the lines provided or a separate journal to write out our key passage multiple times.

I WILL REMEMBER THE LORD'S WORKS; YES, I WILL REMEMBER YOUR ANCIENT WONDERS. I WILL REFLECT ON ALL YOU HAVE DONE AND MEDITATE ON YOUR ACTIONS.

PSALM 77:11–12

_____

_____

_____

_____

_____

_____

_____

_____

_____

_____

See additional tips for memorizing Scripture on page 100.

ACTING IN

WEEK

03

REMEMBRANCE

In God's kindness, He gives us tangible reminders of who He is, what He has done, and how we are to live as His children. Baptism, a table, and the promise of Christ's return all serve as spiritual touchstones for believers so we're never too far from those past experiences that form us in the present and future.

In this week's readings, we will reflect on the practices and actions God has given us to strengthen our experience of His presence in our everyday lives.

WE  REMEMBER YOUR INSTRUCTION

2 KINGS 22:8–13

The Book of the Law Found

8 The high priest Hilkiah told the court secretary Shaphan, "I have found the book of the law in the LORD's temple," and he gave the book to Shaphan, who read it.

9 Then the court secretary Shaphan went to the king and reported, "Your servants have emptied out the silver that was found in the temple and have given it to those doing the work—those who oversee the LORD's temple." 10 Then the court secretary Shaphan told the king, "The priest Hilkiah has given me a book," and Shaphan read it in the presence of the king.

11 When the king heard the words of the book of the law, he tore his clothes. 12 Then he commanded the priest Hilkiah, Ahikam son of Shaphan, Achbor son of Micaiah, the court secretary Shaphan, and the king's servant Asaiah, 13 "Go and inquire of the LORD for me, for the people, and for all Judah about the words in this book that has been found. For great is the LORD's wrath that is kindled against us because our ancestors have not obeyed the words of this book in order to do everything written about us."

2 KINGS 23:1–3

Covenant Renewal

1 So the king sent messengers, and they gathered all the elders of Judah and Jerusalem to him. 2 Then the king went to the LORD's temple with all the men of Judah and all the inhabitants of Jerusalem, as well as the priests and the prophets—all the people from the youngest to the oldest. He read in their hearing all the words of the book of the covenant that had been found in the LORD's temple. 3 Next, the king stood by the pillar and made a covenant in the LORD's presence to follow the LORD and to keep his commands, his decrees, and his statutes with all his heart and with all his soul in order to carry out the words of this covenant that were written in this book; all the people agreed to the covenant.

PSALM 119:55

LORD, I remember your name in the night,
and I obey your instruction.

◗ GOING DEEPER

JOHN 14:23–26

²³ Jesus answered, "If anyone loves me, he will keep my word. My Father will love him, and we will come to him and make our home with him. ²⁴ The one who doesn't love me will not keep my words. The word that you hear is not mine but is from the Father who sent me.

²⁵ "I have spoken these things to you while I remain with you.

²⁶ But the Counselor, the Holy Spirit, whom the Father will send in my name, will teach you all things and remind you of everything I have told you."

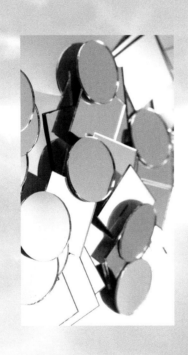

WE REMEMBER YOUR PRESENCE WITH US

DAY 16

The LORD is the one who will go before you. He will be with you.

DEUTERONOMY 31:8

DEUTERONOMY 31:1–8

Joshua Takes Moses's Place

[1] Then Moses continued to speak these words to all Israel, [2] saying, "I am now 120 years old; I can no longer act as your leader. The LORD has told me, 'You will not cross the Jordan.' [3] The LORD your God is the one who will cross ahead of you. He will destroy these nations before you, and you will drive them out. Joshua is the one who will cross ahead of you, as the LORD has said. [4] The LORD will deal with them as he did Sihon and Og, the kings of the Amorites, and their land when he destroyed them. [5] The LORD will deliver them over to you, and you must do to them exactly as I have commanded you. [6] Be strong and courageous; don't be terrified or afraid of them. For the LORD your God is the one who will go with you; he will not leave you or abandon you."

[7] Moses then summoned Joshua and said to him in the sight of all Israel, "Be strong and courageous, for you will go with this people into the land the LORD swore to give to their ancestors. You will enable them to take possession of it. [8] The LORD is the one who will go before you. He will be with you; he will not leave you or abandon you. Do not be afraid or discouraged."

ISAIAH 41:8–10

[8] "But you, Israel, my servant,
Jacob, whom I have chosen,
descendant of Abraham, my friend—
[9] I brought you from the ends of the earth
and called you from its farthest corners.
I said to you: You are my servant;
I have chosen you; I haven't rejected you.
[10] Do not fear, for I am with you;
do not be afraid, for I am your God.
I will strengthen you; I will help you;
I will hold on to you with my righteous right hand."

ISAIAH 43:2

"When you pass through the waters,
I will be with you,
and the rivers will not overwhelm you.
When you walk through the fire,
you will not be scorched,
and the flame will not burn you."

◗ GOING DEEPER

JOHN 14:16–18

[16] "And I will ask the Father, and he will give you another Counselor to be with you forever.

[17] He is the Spirit of truth. The world is unable to receive him because it doesn't see him or know him. But you do know him, because he remains with you and will be in you.

[18] "I will not leave you as orphans; I am coming to you."

NOTES / NOTES

WE REMEMBER YOUR SACRIFICE

"This is my body, which is given for you. Do this in remembrance of me."

LUKE 22:19

LUKE 22:7–23

Preparation for Passover

[7] Then the Day of Unleavened Bread came when the Passover lamb had to be sacrificed. [8] Jesus sent Peter and John, saying, "Go and make preparations for us to eat the Passover."

[9] "Where do you want us to prepare it?" they asked him.

[10] "Listen," he said to them, "when you've entered the city, a man carrying a water jug will meet you. Follow him into the house he enters. [11] Tell the owner of the house, 'The Teacher asks you, "Where is the guest room where I can eat the Passover with my disciples?"' [12] Then he will show you a large, furnished room upstairs. Make the preparations there."

[13] So they went and found it just as he had told them, and they prepared the Passover.

The First Lord's Supper

[14] When the hour came, he reclined at the table, and the apostles with him. [15] Then he said to them, "I have fervently desired to eat this Passover with you before I suffer. [16] For I tell you, I will not eat it again until it is fulfilled in the kingdom of God." [17] Then he took a cup, and after giving thanks, he said, "Take this and share it among yourselves. [18] For I tell you, from now on I will not drink of the fruit of the vine until the kingdom of God comes."

[19] And he took bread, gave thanks, broke it, gave it to them, and said, "This is my body, which is given for you. Do this in remembrance of me."

[20] In the same way he also took the cup after supper and said, "This cup is the new covenant in my blood, which is poured out for you. [21] But look, the hand of the one betraying me is at the table with me. [22] For the Son of Man will go away as it has been determined, but woe to that man by whom he is betrayed!"

[23] So they began to argue among themselves which of them it could be who was going to do it.

1 CORINTHIANS 11:23–26

[23] For I received from the Lord what I also passed on to you: On the night when he was betrayed, the Lord Jesus took bread, [24] and when he had given thanks, broke it, and said, "This is my body, which is for you. Do this in remembrance of me."

[25] In the same way also he took the cup, after supper, and said, "This cup is the new covenant in my blood. Do this, as often as you drink it, in remembrance of me."

[26] For as often as you eat this bread and drink the cup, you proclaim the Lord's death until he comes.

■ GOING DEEPER

HEBREWS 9:3–26

[3] Behind the second curtain was a tent called the most holy place. [4] It had the gold altar of incense and the ark of the covenant, covered with gold on all sides, in which was a gold jar containing the manna, Aaron's staff that budded, and the tablets of the covenant. [5] The cherubim of glory were above the ark overshadowing the mercy seat. It is not possible to speak about these things in detail right now.

[6] With these things prepared like this, the priests enter the first room repeatedly, performing their ministry. [7] But the high priest alone enters the second room, and he does that only once a year, and never without blood, which he offers for himself and for the sins the people had committed in ignorance. [8] The Holy Spirit was making it clear that the way into the most holy place had not yet been disclosed while the first tabernacle was still standing. [9] This is a symbol for the present time, during which gifts and sacrifices are offered that cannot perfect the worshiper's conscience. [10] They are physical regulations and only deal with food, drink, and various washings imposed until the time of the new order.

New Covenant Ministry
[11] But Christ has appeared as a high priest of the good things that have come. In the greater and more perfect tabernacle not made with hands (that is, not of this creation), [12] he entered the most holy place once for all time, not by the blood of goats and calves, but by his own blood, having obtained eternal redemption. [13] For if the blood of goats and bulls and the ashes of a young cow, sprinkling those

who are defiled, sanctify for the purification of the flesh, [14] how much more will the blood of Christ, who through the eternal Spirit offered himself without blemish to God, cleanse our consciences from dead works so that we can serve the living God?

[15] Therefore, he is the mediator of a new covenant, so that those who are called might receive the promise of the eternal inheritance, because a death has taken place for redemption from the transgressions committed under the first covenant. [16] Where a will exists, the death of the one who made it must be established. [17] For a will is valid only when people die, since it is never in effect while the one who made it is living. [18] That is why even the first covenant was inaugurated with blood. [19] For when every command had been proclaimed by Moses to all the people according to the law, he took the blood of calves and goats, along with water, scarlet wool, and hyssop, and sprinkled the scroll itself and all the people, [20] saying, This is the blood of the covenant that God has ordained for you. [21] In the same way, he sprinkled the tabernacle and all the articles of worship with blood. [22] According to the law almost everything is purified with blood, and without the shedding of blood there is no forgiveness.

[23] Therefore, it was necessary for the copies of the things in the heavens to be purified with these sacrifices, but the heavenly things themselves to be purified with better sacrifices than these. [24] For Christ did not enter a sanctuary made with hands (only a model of the true one) but into heaven itself, so that he might now appear in the presence of God for us. [25] He did not do this to offer himself many times, as the high priest enters the sanctuary yearly with the blood of another. [26] Otherwise, he would have had to suffer many times since the foundation of the world. But now he has appeared one time, at the end of the ages, for the removal of sin by the sacrifice of himself.

HEBREWS 10:11–12

[11] Every priest stands day after day ministering and offering the same sacrifices time after time, which can never take away sins. [12] But this man, after offering one sacrifice for sins forever, sat down at the right hand of God.

MARKERS OF REMEMBRANCE IN SCRIPTURE

Throughout both the Old and New Testaments, we see several instances of God's people being called to physical actions of remembrance. These included building memorials, celebrating holy days, keeping records, and establishing shared rhythms to commemorate something God had done. Most involved everyday objects like bread, stones, and water, but each pointed to a deeper spiritual reality.

Included here are some examples of remembrance in both the Old and New Testaments.

OLD TESTAMENT

FEASTS AND HOLY DAYS

- The Passover Feast Ex 12:14–16, 24–28, 43–51
- Festival of Unleavened Bread Ex 12:15–20, 39–42
- The Sabbath Ex 20:8–11
- Festival of Harvest (Pentecost) Ex 23:16
- Festival of Trumpets (Rosh Hashanah) Lv 23:23–25
- Festival of Shelters (Sukkot) Lv 23:33–43
- Purim (Festival of Lots) Est 9

ALTARS, MEMORIALS, AND OBJECTS

- Noah's altar to the Lord Gn 8:20
- Abraham's altars to the Lord Gn 12:7–8; 13:18; 22:9
- Isaac's altar to the Lord Gn 26:25
- Jacob's altar to God Gn 33:20; 35:1, 7
- Moses's altars to the Lord Ex 17:8–16; 20:24–26; 24:4–6
- New stones of the law and an altar to the Lord Dt 27:1–8
- Tassels for remembrance Nm 15:37–41
- Joshua's altar to the Lord Jos 8:30
- Israel's memorial stones Jos 4
- Gideon's altar to the Lord Jdg 6:24
- Samuel's stone marker 1Sm 7:12
- Saul's altar to the Lord 1Sm 14:35
- David's altar to the Lord 2Sm 24:25

COMMITMENT CEREMONIES

- The Israelites' consecration at Gilgal Jos 5:1–9
- Renewed commitment to the law Jos 8:30–35

WRITTEN RECORDS

- Books of remembrance Est 6:1; Mal 3:16
- Court historians 2Sm 20:24; 1Ch 18:15

NEW TESTAMENT

CEREMONIAL REMINDERS

- The Lord's Supper Lk 22:19
- Baptism Rm 6:1–11

REGULAR PRACTICES

- Acts of service Mk 14:6–9

WRITTEN RECORDS

- Letters and apostolic teaching 1Co 1:17; 2Pt 1:12–15

WE REMEMBER  YOUR RESURRECTION

LUKE 24:1–9

Resurrection Morning

[1] On the first day of the week, very early in the morning, they came to the tomb, bringing the spices they had prepared. [2] They found the stone rolled away from the tomb. [3] They went in but did not find the body of the Lord Jesus. [4] While they were perplexed about this, suddenly two men stood by them in dazzling clothes. [5] So the women were terrified and bowed down to the ground.

"Why are you looking for the living among the dead?" asked the men. [6] "He is not here, but he has risen! Remember how he spoke to you when he was still in Galilee, [7] saying, 'It is necessary that the Son of Man be betrayed into the hands of sinful men, be crucified, and rise on the third day'?" [8] And they remembered his words.

[9] Returning from the tomb, they reported all these things to the Eleven and to all the rest.

2 CORINTHIANS 4:14

For we know that the one who raised the Lord Jesus will also raise us with Jesus and present us with you.

ROMANS 6:1–11

The New Life in Christ

[1] What should we say then? Should we continue in sin so that grace may multiply? [2] Absolutely not! How can we who died to sin still live in it? [3] Or are you unaware that all of us who were baptized into Christ Jesus were baptized into his death? [4] Therefore we were buried with him by baptism into death, in order that, just as Christ was raised from the dead by the glory of the Father, so we too may walk in newness of life. [5] For if we have been united with him in the likeness of his death, we will certainly also be in the likeness of his resurrection. [6] For we know that our old self was crucified with him so that the body ruled by sin might be rendered powerless so that we may no longer be enslaved to sin, [7] since a person who has died is freed from sin. [8] Now if we died with Christ, we believe that we will also live with him, [9] because we know that Christ, having been raised from the dead, will not die again. Death no longer rules over him. [10] For the death he died, he died to sin once for all time; but the life he lives, he lives to God. [11] So, you too consider yourselves dead to sin and alive to God in Christ Jesus.

◗ GOING DEEPER

1 CORINTHIANS 15:1–28, 50–57

Resurrection Essential to the Gospel

[1] Now I want to make clear for you, brothers and sisters, the gospel I preached to you, which you received, on which you have taken your stand [2] and by which you are being saved, if you hold to the message I preached to you—unless you believed in vain. [3] For I passed on to you as most important what I also received: that Christ died for our sins according to the Scriptures, [4] that he was buried, that he was raised on the third day according to the Scriptures, [5] and that he appeared to Cephas, then to the Twelve. [6] Then he appeared

to over five hundred brothers and sisters at one time; most of them are still alive, but some have fallen asleep. [7] Then he appeared to James, then to all the apostles. [8] Last of all, as to one born at the wrong time, he also appeared to me.

[9] For I am the least of the apostles, not worthy to be called an apostle, because I persecuted the church of God. [10] But by the grace of God I am what I am, and his grace toward me was not in vain. On the contrary, I worked harder than any of them, yet not I, but the grace of God that was with me. [11] Whether, then, it is I or they, so we proclaim and so you have believed.

Resurrection Essential to the Faith

[12] Now if Christ is proclaimed as raised from the dead, how can some of you say, "There is no resurrection of the dead"? [13] If there is no resurrection of the dead, then not even Christ has been raised; [14] and if Christ has not been raised, then our proclamation is in vain, and so is your faith. [15] Moreover, we are found to be false witnesses about God, because we have testified wrongly about God that he raised up Christ—whom he did not raise up, if in fact the dead are not raised. [16] For if the dead are not raised, not even Christ has been raised. [17] And if Christ has not been raised, your faith is worthless; you are still in your sins. [18] Those, then, who have fallen asleep in Christ have also perished. [19] If we have put our hope in Christ for this life only, we should be pitied more than anyone.

Christ's Resurrection Guarantees Ours

[20] But as it is, Christ has been raised from the dead, the firstfruits of those who have fallen asleep. [21] For since death came through a man, the resurrection of the dead also comes through a man. [22] For just as in Adam all die, so also in Christ all will be made alive.

[23] But each in his own order: Christ, the firstfruits; afterward, at his coming, those who belong to Christ. [24] Then comes the end, when he hands over the kingdom to God the Father, when he abolishes all rule and all authority and power. [25] For he must reign until he puts all his enemies under his feet. [26] The last enemy to be abolished is death. [27] For God has put everything under his feet. Now when it says "everything" is put under him, it is obvious that he who puts everything

under him is the exception. [28] When everything is subject to Christ, then the Son himself will also be subject to the one who subjected everything to him, so that God may be all in all.

…

Victorious Resurrection

[50] What I am saying, brothers and sisters, is this: Flesh and blood cannot inherit the kingdom of God, nor can corruption inherit incorruption. [51] Listen, I am telling you a mystery: We will not all fall asleep, but we will all be changed, [52] in a moment, in the twinkling of an eye, at the last trumpet. For the trumpet will sound, and the dead will be raised incorruptible, and we will be changed. [53] For this corruptible body must be clothed with incorruptibility, and this mortal body must be clothed with immortality. [54] When this corruptible body is clothed with incorruptibility, and this mortal body is clothed with immortality, then the saying that is written will take place:

Death has been swallowed up in victory.
[55] Where, death, is your victory?
Where, death, is your sting?

[56] The sting of death is sin, and the power of sin is the law. [57] But thanks be to God, who gives us the victory through our Lord Jesus Christ!

NOTES / NOTES

FOR IF WE BELIEVE THAT JESUS DIED AND ROSE AGAIN, IN THE SAME WAY, THROUGH JESUS, GOD WILL BRING WITH HIM THOSE WHO HAVE FALLEN ASLEEP.

1 THESSALONIANS 4:14

WE REMEMBER YOU ARE COMING AGAIN

ISAIAH 65:17–25

A New Creation

17 "For I will create new heavens and a new earth;
the past events will not be remembered or come
   to mind.
18 Then be glad and rejoice forever
in what I am creating;
for I will create Jerusalem to be a joy
and its people to be a delight.
19 I will rejoice in Jerusalem
and be glad in my people.
The sound of weeping and crying
will no longer be heard in her.
20 In her, a nursing infant will no longer live
only a few days,
or an old man not live out his days.
Indeed, the one who dies at a hundred years old
will be mourned as a young man,
and the one who misses a hundred years
will be considered cursed.
21 People will build houses and live in them;

they will plant vineyards and eat their fruit.
22 They will not build and others live in them;
they will not plant and others eat.
For my people's lives will be
like the lifetime of a tree.
My chosen ones will fully enjoy
the work of their hands.
23 They will not labor without success
or bear children destined for disaster,
for they will be a people blessed by the Lord
along with their descendants.
24 Even before they call, I will answer;
while they are still speaking, I will hear.
25 The wolf and the lamb will feed together,
and the lion will eat straw like cattle,
but the serpent's food will be dust!
They will not do what is evil or destroy
on my entire holy mountain,"
says the Lord.

NOTES / NOTES

1 THESSALONIANS 4:13–18
The Comfort of Christ's Coming

13 We do not want you to be uninformed, brothers and sisters, concerning those who are asleep, so that you will not grieve like the rest, who have no hope. 14 For if we believe that Jesus died and rose again, in the same way, through Jesus, God will bring with him those who have fallen asleep. 15 For we say this to you by a word from the Lord: We who are still alive at the Lord's coming will certainly not precede those who have fallen asleep. 16 For the Lord himself will descend from heaven with a shout, with the archangel's voice, and with the trumpet of God, and the dead in Christ will rise first. 17 Then we who are still alive, who are left, will be caught up together with them in the clouds to meet the Lord in the air, and so we will always be with the Lord. 18 Therefore encourage one another with these words.

◆ **GOING DEEPER**

REVELATION 22:6–21
The Time Is Near

6 Then he said to me, "These words are faithful and true. The Lord, the God of the spirits of the prophets, has sent his angel to show his servants what must soon take place."

7 "Look, I am coming soon! Blessed is the one who keeps the words of the prophecy of this book."

8 I, John, am the one who heard and saw these things. When I heard and saw them, I fell down to worship at the feet of the angel who had shown them to me. 9 But he said to me, "Don't do that! I am a fellow servant with you, your brothers the prophets, and those who keep the words of this book. Worship God!"

10 Then he said to me, "Don't seal up the words of the prophecy of this book, because the time is near. 11 Let the unrighteous go on in unrighteousness; let the filthy still be filthy; let the righteous go on in righteousness; let the holy still be holy."

[12] "Look, I am coming soon, and my reward is with me to repay each person according to his work. [13] I am the Alpha and the Omega, the first and the last, the beginning and the end.

[14] Blessed are those who wash their robes, so that they may have the right to the tree of life and may enter the city by the gates. [15] Outside are the dogs, the sorcerers, the sexually immoral, the murderers, the idolaters, and everyone who loves and practices falsehood.

[16] I, Jesus, have sent my angel to attest these things to you for the churches. I am the Root and descendant of David, the bright morning star."

[17] Both the Spirit and the bride say, "Come!" Let anyone who hears, say, "Come!" Let the one who is thirsty come. Let the one who desires take the water of life freely.

[18] I testify to everyone who hears the words of the prophecy of this book: If anyone adds to them, God will add to him the plagues that are written in this book. [19] And if anyone takes away from the words of the book of this prophecy, God will take away his share of the tree of life and the holy city, which are written about in this book.

[20] He who testifies about these things says, "Yes, I am coming soon."

Amen! Come, Lord Jesus!

[21] The grace of the Lord Jesus be with everyone. Amen.

RESPONSE / RESPONSE

Over the last two weeks, we've practiced different rhythms of remembrance to help surrender the areas of our life where we want to remember what is true of God and how He remembers us. Reflect on the ways you have practiced remembering and what the discipline meant to you. If you didn't get the chance to practice the way you planned, use this space to think about which reading days were impactful. Then, consider how you want to incorporate this discipline into your life beyond this plan.

Which practice was familiar, and which was challenging for me? Why?

⬭ KNOW THE STORY

⬭ WRITE DOWN YOUR STORY

⬭ SHARE STORIES IN COMMUNITY

⬭ MARK A MILESTONE

⬭ OTHER (IF YOU CAME UP WITH YOUR OWN):

_____

What did God do in my heart, mind, and life through this practice?

What do I want to incorporate into my life beyond this plan?

GRACE DAY

"WHEN YOU PASS THROUGH THE WATERS, I WILL BE WITH YOU, AND THE RIVERS WILL NOT OVERWHELM YOU. WHEN YOU WALK THROUGH THE FIRE, YOU WILL NOT BE SCORCHED, AND THE FLAME WILL NOT BURN YOU."

ISAIAH 43:2

Take this day to catch up on your reading, pray, and rest in the presence of the Lord.

WEEK THREE / DAY TWENTY

I WILL REMEMBER THE LORD'S WORKS; YES, I WILL REMEMBER YOUR ANCIENT WONDERS. I WILL REFLECT ON ALL YOU HAVE DONE AND MEDITATE ON YOUR ACTIONS.

PSALM 77:11–12

Scripture is God-breathed and true. When we memorize it, we carry the good news of Jesus with us wherever we go.

Throughout this plan we have been committing our key passage to memory by using different Scripture memorization tools to fill our hearts and minds with the truth of God's Word in new ways.

In a journal or on a separate piece of paper, start by copying the verse a few times. Then, fill in the blanks on the following page. Push yourself to fill in the blanks from memory, and keep going even if you need to look back at this page for a hint.

I WILL _____ THE LORD'S
WORKS; ____, I WILL REMEMBER
YOUR ANCIENT _____. I WILL
REFLECT ON ALL YOU HAVE _____
AND MEDITATE ON YOUR ACTIONS.

_____ 77:11–12

I WILL REMEMBER THE LORD'S
_____; YES, I WILL _____
YOUR ANCIENT WONDERS. I WILL
_____ ON ALL ____ HAVE DONE
____ MEDITATE ON YOUR _____.

PSALM ___:11–12

I _____ REMEMBER THE _____
WORKS; YES, I WILL REMEMBER
YOUR _____ WONDERS. I WILL
REFLECT ON ____ YOU HAVE DONE
AND _____ ON YOUR ACTIONS.

PSALM 77:____

See additional tips for memorizing Scripture on page 100.

BENEDICTION

"REMEMBER WHAT HAPPENED LONG AGO, FOR I AM GOD, AND THERE IS NO OTHER; I AM GOD, AND NO ONE IS LIKE ME."

ISAIAH 46:9

Tips for Memorizing Scripture

At She Reads Truth, we believe Scripture memorization is an important discipline in your walk with God. Committing God's Truth to memory means He can minister to us—and we can minister to others—through His Word no matter where we are. As you approach the Weekly Truth passage in this book, try these memorization tips to see which techniques work best for you!

STUDY IT

Study the passage in its biblical context and ask yourself a few questions before you begin to memorize it: What does this passage say? What does it mean? How would I say this in my own words? What does it teach me about God? Understanding what the passage means helps you know why it is important to carry it with you wherever you go.

Break the passage into smaller sections, memorizing a phrase at a time.

PRAY IT

Use the passage you are memorizing as a prompt for prayer.

WRITE IT

Dedicate a notebook to Scripture memorization and write the passage over and over again.

Diagram the passage after you write it out. Place a square around the verbs, underline the nouns, and circle any adjectives or adverbs. Say the passage aloud several times, emphasizing the verbs as you repeat it. Then do the same thing again with the nouns, then the adjectives and adverbs.

Write out the first letter of each word in the passage somewhere you can reference it throughout the week as you work on your memorization.

Use a whiteboard to write out the passage. Erase a few words at a time as you continue to repeat it aloud. Keep erasing parts of the passage until you have it all committed to memory.

CREATE

If you can, make up a tune for the passage to sing as you go about your day, or try singing it to the tune of a favorite song.

Sketch the passage, visualizing what each phrase would look like in the form of a picture. Or, try using calligraphy or altering the style of your handwriting as you write it out.

Use hand signals or signs to come up with associations for each word or phrase and repeat the movements as you practice.

SAY IT

Repeat the passage out loud to yourself as you are going through the rhythm of your day—getting ready, pouring your coffee, waiting in traffic, or making dinner.

Listen to the passage read aloud to you.

Record a voice memo on your phone and listen to it throughout the day or play it on an audio Bible.

SHARE IT

Memorize the passage with a friend, family member, or mentor. Spontaneously challenge each other to recite the passage, or pick a time to review your passage and practice saying it from memory together.

Send the passage as an encouraging text to a friend, testing yourself as you type to see how much you have memorized so far.

KEEP AT IT!

Set reminders on your phone to prompt you to practice your passage.

Purchase a She Reads Truth 12 Card Set or keep a stack of note cards with Scripture you are memorizing by your bed. Practice reciting what you've memorized previously before you go to sleep, ending with the passages you are currently learning. If you wake up in the middle of the night, review them again instead of grabbing your phone. Read them out loud before you get out of bed in the morning.

CSB BOOK ABBREVIATIONS

OLD TESTAMENT

GN Genesis

EX Exodus

LV Leviticus

NM Numbers

DT Deuteronomy

JOS Joshua

JDG Judges

RU Ruth

1SM 1 Samuel

2SM 2 Samuel

1KG 1 Kings

2KG 2 Kings

1CH 1 Chronicles

2CH 2 Chronicles

EZR Ezra

NEH Nehemiah

EST Esther

JB Job

PS Psalms

PR Proverbs

EC Ecclesiastes

SG Song of Solomon

IS Isaiah

JR Jeremiah

LM Lamentations

EZK Ezekiel

DN Daniel

HS Hosea

JL Joel

AM Amos

OB Obadiah

JNH Jonah

MC Micah

NAH Nahum

HAB Habakkuk

ZPH Zephaniah

HG Haggai

ZCH Zechariah

MAL Malachi

NEW TESTAMENT

MT Matthew

MK Mark

LK Luke

JN John

AC Acts

RM Romans

1CO 1 Corinthians

2CO 2 Corinthians

GL Galatians

EPH Ephesians

PHP Philippians

COL Colossians

1TH 1 Thessalonians

2TH 2 Thessalonians

1TM 1 Timothy

2TM 2 Timothy

TI Titus

PHM Philemon

HEB Hebrews

JMS James

1PT 1 Peter

2PT 2 Peter

1JN 1 John

2JN 2 John

3JN 3 John

JD Jude

RV Revelation

BIBLIOGRAPHY

Jones, Spencer A. "Memory," in *Lexham Theological Wordbook*, edited by Douglas Mangum et al. Bellingham: Lexham Press, 2014.

You just spent 21 days in the Word of God!

MY FAVORITE DAY OF
THIS READING PLAN:

ONE THING I LEARNED
ABOUT GOD:

WHAT WAS GOD DOING IN
MY LIFE DURING THIS STUDY?

HOW DID I FIND DELIGHT IN GOD'S WORD?

WHAT DID I LEARN THAT I WANT TO SHARE
WITH SOMEONE ELSE?

A SPECIFIC PASSAGE OR VERSE THAT
ENCOURAGED ME:

A SPECIFIC PASSAGE OR VERSE THAT
CHALLENGED AND CONVICTED ME: